HANDEL
Air and Rondo
for oboe and piano

edited and arranged by
EVELYN ROTHWELL

CHESTER MUSIC

AIR

**Edited & Arranged for Oboe
by Evelyn Rothwell**

HANDEL

RONDO

OBOE

HANDEL

Allegro ma non presto

AIR

OBOE

Edited & Arranged for Oboe
by Evelyn Rothwell

HANDEL

RONDO

HANDEL

CH01572